Mother
Teresa

Iris Howden

Published in association with The Basic Skills Agency

Hodder & Stoughton
A MEMBER OF THE HODDER HEADLINE GROUP

Acknowledgements

Photos: pp. 3, 19 © Corbis-Bettmann, pp. 5, 11, 14 © Associated Press/Topham, p. 8 © Camera Press, pp. 16, 27 © Popperfoto/Reuter.
Cover photo: © Corbis-Bettmann.

Orders: please contact Bookpoint Ltd, 39 Milton Park, Abingdon, Oxon OX14 4TD. Telephone: (44) 01235 400414, Fax: (44) 01235 400454. Lines are open from 9.00–6.00, Monday to Saturday, with a 24 hour message answering service. Email address: orders@bookpoint.co.uk

British Library Cataloguing in Publication Data
A catalogue record for this title is available from The British Library

ISBN 0 340 71157 4

First published 1998
Impression number 10 9 8 7 6 5 4 3 2
Year 2002 2001 2000 1999

Typeset by Fakenham Photosetting Ltd, Fakenham, Norfolk.
Printed in Great Britain for Hodder & Stoughton Educational, a division of Hodder Headline Plc, 338 Euston Road, London NW1 3BH by Redwood Books, Trowbridge, Wiltshire.

Contents

1 Mother Teresa

Mother Teresa is one of the best known
women of our time.
She has often been seen on TV
with world leaders, kings and queens.

When she went to Rome, she met Princess Diana.
It was odd to see them side by side.
The Princess was tall and smartly dressed.
Mother Teresa was tiny and bent.
Her dark face was lined with age.
She wore a simple blue and white sari.

She has mixed with the rich and famous
but has spent her life living amongst
the poorest of the poor.

Much has been written about her work.
Very little is known about the woman herself.
The press make up names for her.
They call her 'The Saint of the Gutters'
or the 'Angel of Calcutta'.
She never spoke about her life
or read any of the books about her.

2 Early Days

Mother Teresa was born on
26 August 1910 in Albania.
Her real name was Agnes Bojaxhiu.
The family pet name for her was 'flower bud'.
They called her that because she was
so plump and pink!

She had a younger brother and a sister.
They lived in a large house with
a nice garden. Agnes was a good child.
Her brother said she was the only one
who never stole the jam.
But she did not tell tales about him
when he did.

Her father was a builder.
He was a kind man who gave money
to the poor.
Her mother hated to see waste.
She would turn off the lights after tea.
'You children can chat in the dark,'
she'd say.
When Agnes was seven her father died.
The family was not so well off.
Money was now hard to come by.
Her mother sold carpets to keep the family.

She spent a lot of time at the church.
Agnes went with her.
Their priest would read out letters from nuns
working at a mission school in India.
They wrote about their work there.
When Agnes was only 12 she knew
that she wanted to become a nun.
She waited six years until she was old enough.

At 18 she went to an abbey in Ireland.
She spent two months there learning English.
Then she sailed for India.
This was in November 1928.

She went first to a mission school.
It was in a hill town where rich people
went in summer to get away from the heat.
Agnes learned to speak the Indian languages,
Bengali and Hindi.
She took her first vows on 24 March 1931.
The new name she chose was Sister Teresa.

Her first job was at a school.
She taught there for a few years.
Later on she became the head of the school.
Then she was known as Mother Teresa.
People who knew her say she was a hard worker.
She was gentle but full of fun.
She made her classes come alive.

Mother Teresa meeting the Pope.

3 An Inner Command

It was wartime. Food was in short supply.
Many hundreds of people came to Calcutta.
They lay in the streets, dying of hunger.
Mother Teresa had to pass these poor people
every day on her way to work.
She said she heard 'an inner command'.
It was God telling her to help them.

She wrote to the Pope to ask if she could
leave her job at the convent school.
Mother Teresa had to give up her vows.
She was given a year to try working
in the slums.
She went to Patna to learn first aid skills
with the Little Sisters of the Poor.
Then she was ready to start her life's work.

When she left the convent she had only
five rupees.
All she owned in the world was three saris.
They were white with a blue border.
She asked her priest to bless them.
The convent gave her some pots and pans,
but they would not give her money.
She had to beg for everything she needed.
Mother Teresa has always taken gifts
of money for her work.

4 Her Work Begins

In February 1949 Mother Teresa
opened a school in Calcutta.
It was on the top floor of a house.
She had only a few chairs and packing cases
to use as tables.
She taught the children letters
by drawing them in the dust with a stick.

Two of her ex-pupils came to join her.
One was Sister Agnes.
She went to train as a teacher.
Sister Magdalena became a doctor.
Soon Mother Teresa had ten young women
to help her.
Over the next two years this number
grew to 30.

By this time Mother Teresa had moved
to what was called 'The Motherhouse'.
It has been her headquarters ever since.
It was to become known world wide.

Mother Teresa helping the sick and the poor.

The sisters got up at 5.30 to pray.
At 8.00 they would go out in pairs
into the slums.
Some worked in schools, others in clinics.
They would come back at noon for lunch.
There was more work in the afternoon.
Then supper, prayers and bed at 10.00.
It was a hard life.
Often Mother Teresa had to walk home.
She had given her tram fare away.

Mother Teresa made sure the sisters
looked after their own health.
They could not afford to be ill.
The sisters went around in pairs
in case of trouble.
They often had to pick up people
they found lying ill in the streets.

Some of these people were lepers.
No-one would help those who had
this terrible disease. It made
their fingers and toes rot and drop off.

People were afraid to touch lepers
in case they got the disease.
The hospitals would not take them in.
Often their own families left them to die.

5 Her Work Grows

In 1963 the Brothers of Charity was founded.
They were male helpers who took over the work
with the lepers.
They set up a radio repair shop to train them.
The Brothers built villages where
they could live.
They started farms to help people
learn skills.

The Brothers worked with young men and boys.
Some of these were homeless or on drugs.
The Brothers did not wear a uniform.
They felt it might put people off.

Mother Teresa's work grew fast.
By the end of the 1960s she had set up
25 houses in India.
She ran day centres, schools,
night shelters and clinics.

In India there were many children
who had no parents.
Mother Teresa opened homes for them.
She took in children whose parents could not
afford to keep them.
No child was ever turned away.
She also took in girls who were pregnant.

The 'Brothers of Charity' at work.

6 Homes for the Dying

Once when she was on a tram, Mother Teresa
saw a poor man lying on the pavement.
It was the rainy season.
He was soaking wet.
When she came back she stopped
to see how he was.
He was still there, lying with his head
in a pool of water. He was dead.

Many people in India died in the streets.
Mother Teresa made up her mind
to set up homes for the dying.
These would be places where people
could be looked after and die in peace.

She opened the first one in a local temple.
Local people were upset by this.
They thought she would try to turn people
away from the Hindu religion and
make them into Christians.

A police chief went to look at the home.
When he saw her remove maggots
from someone's face he said,
'This woman is a saint'.

In the 1970s homes began to open abroad.
Mother Teresa went where help was needed.
By the 1980s there were lots of homes
in many different countries.
Some dealt with new problems such as AIDS.

Mother Teresa meeting the Queen.

7 World Fame

Mother Teresa was known all over the world.
Some of the airlines gave her free travel.
Her bags were often first off the plane.
A car would wait outside for her.
Her house in Delhi had been opened
by the Prime Minister himself.
She was on the best of terms with
all the VIPs in Calcutta.

By now she knew many Heads of State.
Royalty were counted as friends.
She could ring the President of the USA
or of Russia and ask for help.
Someone once called her
'the most powerful woman in the world'.

The Pope also did her many favours.
After a visit to India he left behind
a new white car as a gift for her.
Mother Teresa used it as a raffle prize.

Mother Teresa with the Nobel Peace Prize.

Mother Teresa won the Nobel Peace Prize
in 1979.
She saw that it was worth a lot of money.
She got masses of publicity – and she used it.
She asked the Swedish people
to cancel the state banquet.
To give the money instead,
'to those who really need a meal!'
After they read this in the paper
people sent in money for her homes.
Children even gave her their pocket money.

Awards have been heaped upon her.
In 1962 she was the first non-Indian to win
their top award.
In Britain the Queen gave her the O.M. medal.
She was named Woman of the Year many times.
Her head was on some stamps in Sweden.
She had a tulip named after her in Holland.

But in spite of all these prizes,
Mother Teresa did not enjoy public life.
She was a shy person by nature.
She never asked for anything for herself.
All the cash she raised was for the poor.

She hated spending time in meetings.
That took her away from her 'real work'.
She often worked late into the night
writing letters and doing her paper work.
Mother Teresa had many helpers world-wide.
She liked to keep in touch with them.

8 Her Final Years

All this hard work took its toll on a woman
who was getting old.
When she was 73 she fell ill.
She had to go into hospital
for the first time.
Messages came in from all over the world.
The King and Queen of Belgium came
to visit her.

Later on she had a pacemaker fitted.
She wanted to step down, but the sisters
begged her to stay on as their leader.
Her health was not good.
Many people think she should have
retired then.

Mother Teresa went on working
until she was well into her 80s.
Now people began to ask questions
about her work.
Some felt her ideas were out of date.
Some thought she should share control
of the homes.
Others felt she should keep a better check
on the money.

They said that she had an old-fashioned
idea of charity.
That her homes gave only low-level care.
She should do more to prevent illness.

One of the main issues was that of abortion.
Mother Teresa was against it.
She also thought that birth control was wrong.
Others thought it was needed.
There were far too many people in India.

People will argue about these things
for years to come.
Most of her fans regard her as a saint.
For over 50 years she gave hope
to thousands of poor people.
Many of them would have died without her care.

Mother Teresa was a simple woman.
She kept a simple faith all her life.
Everything she did was for others.
She spoke of herself as being:
'only a pencil in the hands of God'.

The card she gave to visitors sums up
her beliefs.
It said:
>The fruit of Silence is Prayer
>The fruit of Prayer is Faith
>The fruit of Faith is Love
>The fruit of Love is Service
>The fruit of Service is Peace.

9 Her Death

Mother Teresa died on 5 September 1997.
Her heart gave out. She was 87 years old.
Her death came five days after
the death of Princess Diana.

It was strange. Two women who had given
so much love to the world had died
in the same week.

As one priest said:
'They had met in life and become friends.
Now they are joined in death.'

Mother Teresa was given a state funeral.
Some of her friends said she would have hated
all the fuss – and the high cost.
But people wanted to show their respect.

They queued for hours to see her in church.
She lay in a simple white coffin.
The flag of India was draped over it.
A glass cover had been fitted
– so the crowd could see her face.

On the day of the funeral her coffin
was put on a gun carriage.
It had been used at Ghandi's funeral.
50,000 people lined the three mile route.
Women threw masses of flower petals.

At the service, the poorest of the poor
mixed with VIPs from many lands.
Hilary Clinton, wife of the US President came.
Queen Noor of Jordan was there.
Gifts for Mother Teresa were laid by
a prisoner, a leper, a deaf man and an orphan.
Others were given by a hospice worker,
a brother and a sister from her order.

Lessons were read in English, Hindi and Bengali.
People from seven religions took part.

After this grand funeral,
Mother Teresa was laid to rest.
There was a simple burial at her HQ.
Only her nuns and a few priests were there.
The sister who took over from her as head
of the order spoke for them all.

She said that Mother Teresa had cared for:
'The hungry, the thirsty, the sick and the dying,
the orphans and lepers.
Those with broken bodies, broken minds
and broken hearts.'

The woman they called 'The Little Mother'
had gone.
But her work will live on.

Mother Teresa meeting Princess Diana.